Colors and Stones
Stones and Colors

Ori Oasis
OrisOasis.com/OriKids

NOTE TO PARENTS

My spiritual path has always been a big part of my life. So it was only natural that when I became a mother, I would want to share that part of my life with my children as well. In my search, I have found plenty of beautiful children's books. But found it impossible to find one that incorporates spirituality with the basic things a child must learn. I am not saying one or more is not out there but as of yet, it has not cross my path. So I decided to create my own. Much to my surprise, my family and friends not only loved the idea, but encouraged me to share it with the world. Whether this is the first of its kind, I do not know. My only desire is that after this, more books like these will be readily available for those who seek them.

Dedication

To all the metaphysical children, looking to quickly remember the knowledge they once knew. And to their metaphysical family members, seeking to aide them in their earthly journey.

ACKNOWLEDGMENTS

To loved ones near and far who are guiding me from the other
side,
To the love of my life for always allowing room for my creativity
to flourish and grow,
To our boys for always inspiring me to do more,
To my soul sister for helping me expand my dreams further than I
could even imagine,
And to all, whether great or small, that have encouraged me in
their own way,
Thank you for being there for me.
Ori

COLOR IS WHAT WE SEE WHEN A LIGHT SOURCE
TOUCHES OUR EYES.

A STONE IS A SOLID HARD PIECE OF EARTH.

EACH STONE HAS A DIFFERENT KIND OF ENERGY.

LET'S LEARN COLORS WITH STONES, WHILE LEARNING THE STONE'S ENERGY.

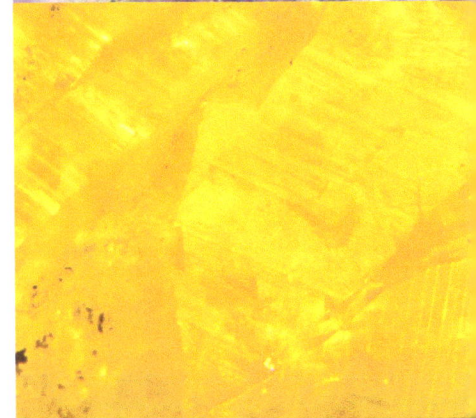

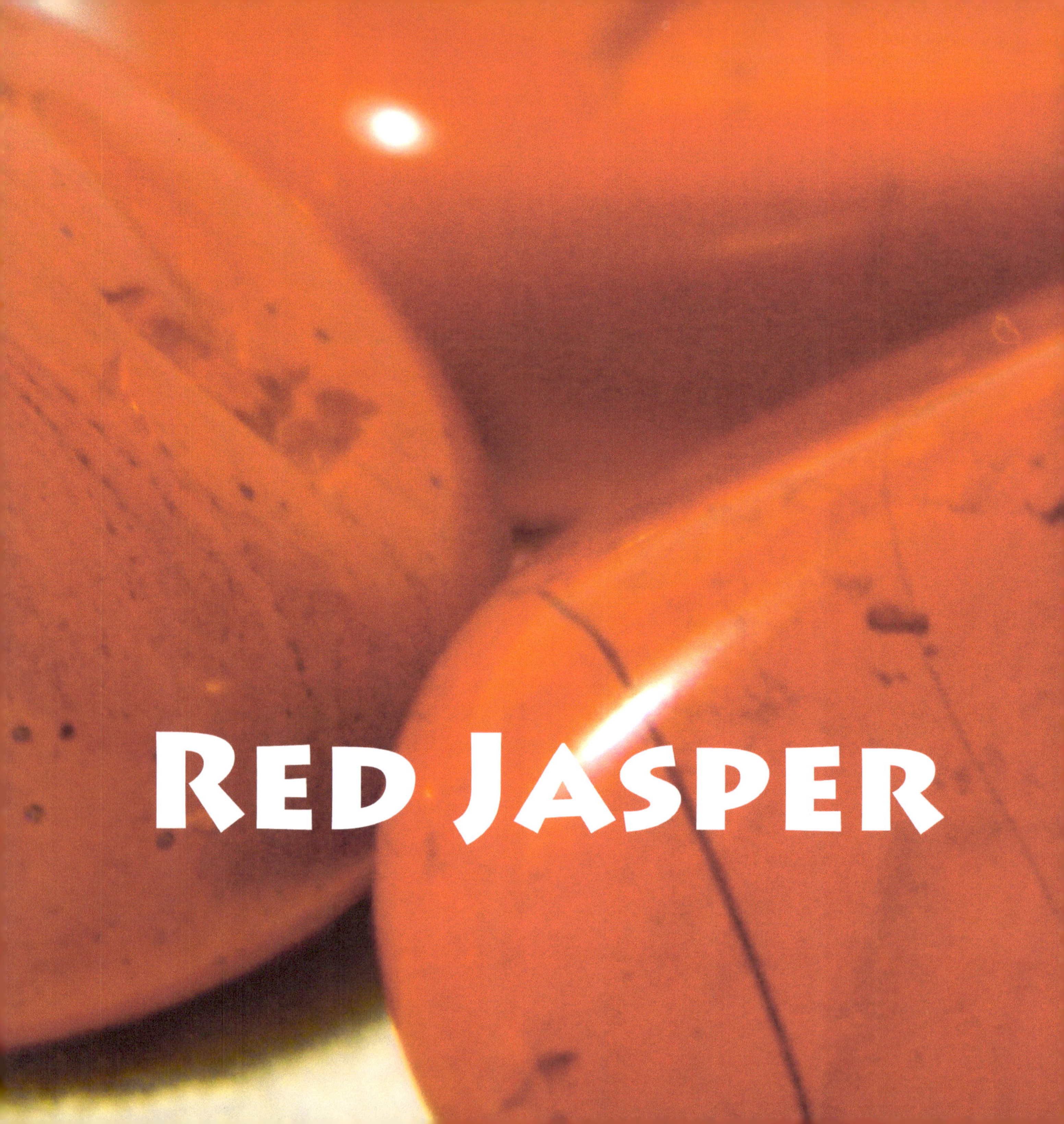
RED JASPER

RED JASPER IS MOSTLY THE COLOR RED.

IT WILL HELP YOU FEEL BETTER WHEN YOU ARE SCARED.

IS THERE ANYTHING THAT SCARES YOU?

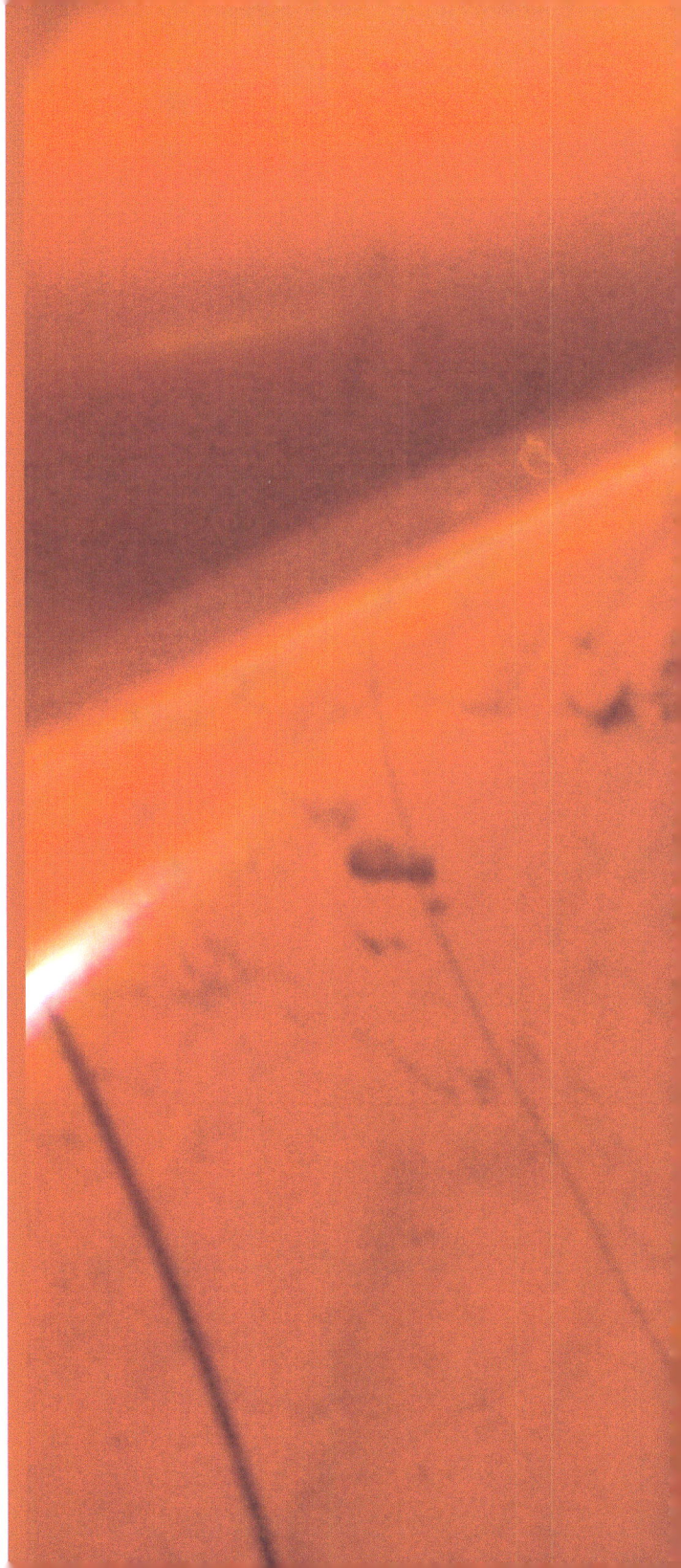

CITRINE

Citrine is the color **yellow**.

Hold it close and it will give you energy.

Can you name foods that give you energy?

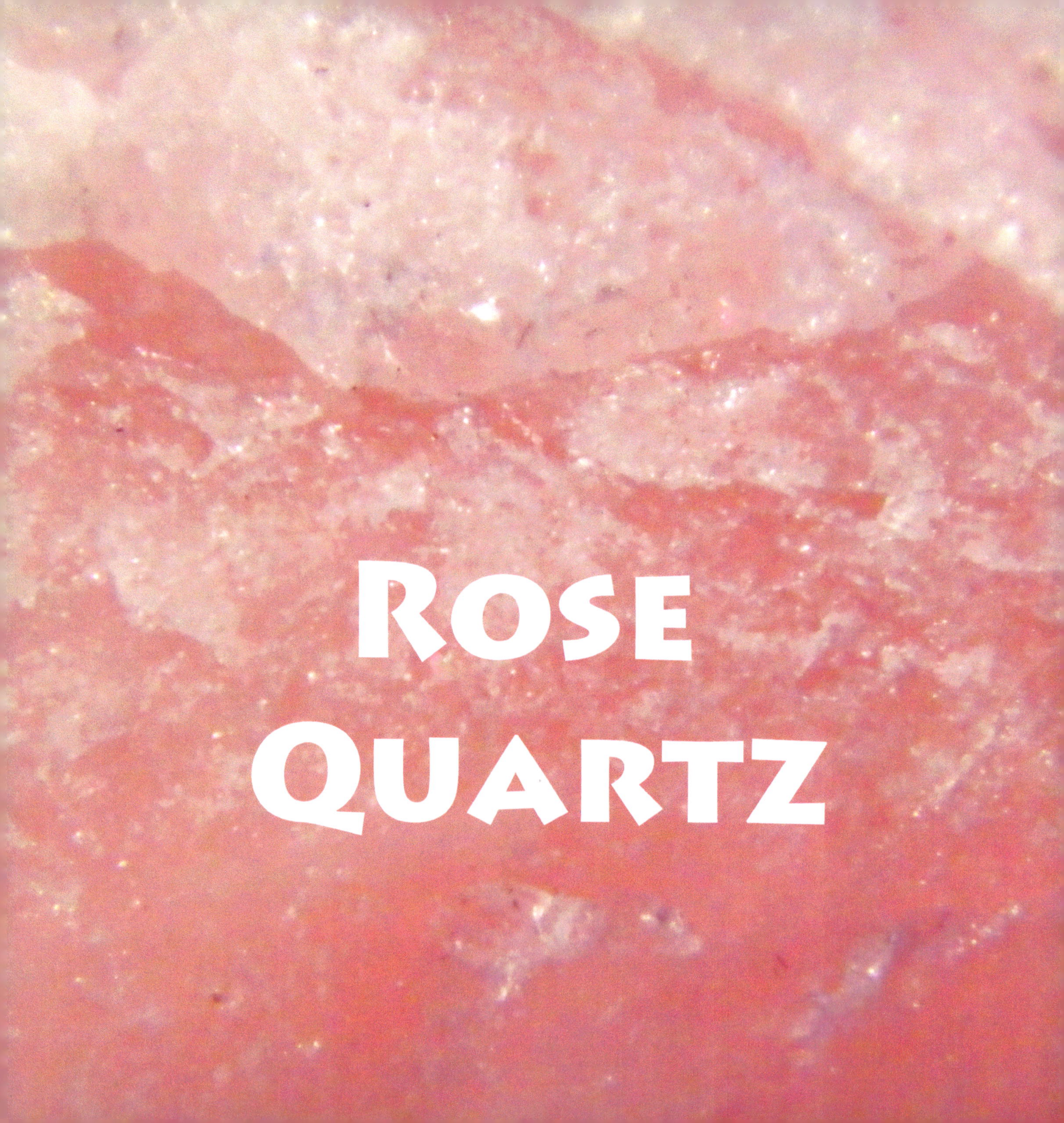
Rose
Quartz

Rose quartz is
the color pink.

Put it close to you,
to feel loved.

Can you name someone
that makes you
feel loved?

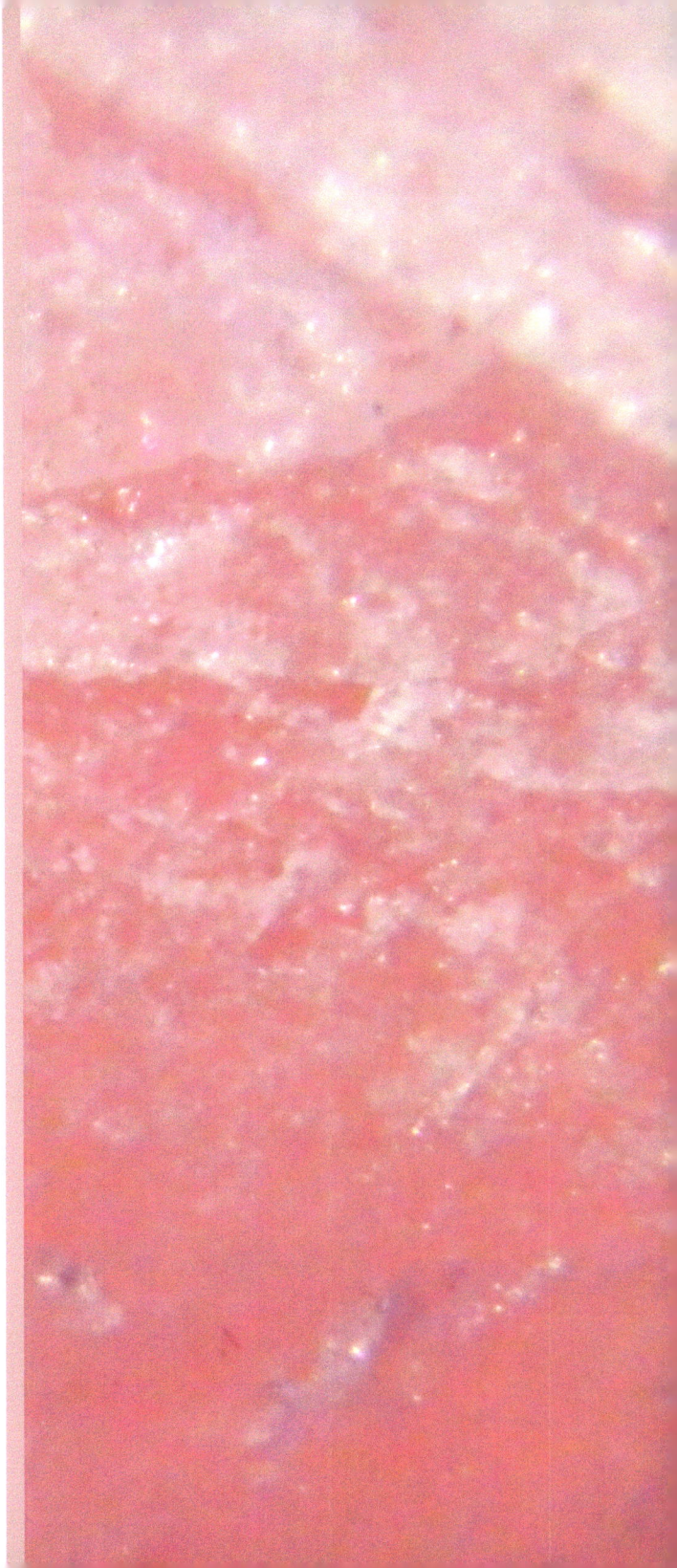

JADE

Jade is mostly the color green.

You can use it to bring you good luck.

What else can you use for good luck?

AMETHYST

AMETHYST IS THE COLOR **PURPLE**.

IT CAN HELP YOU THINK BETTER.

WHAT DO YOU LIKE TO THINK ABOUT?

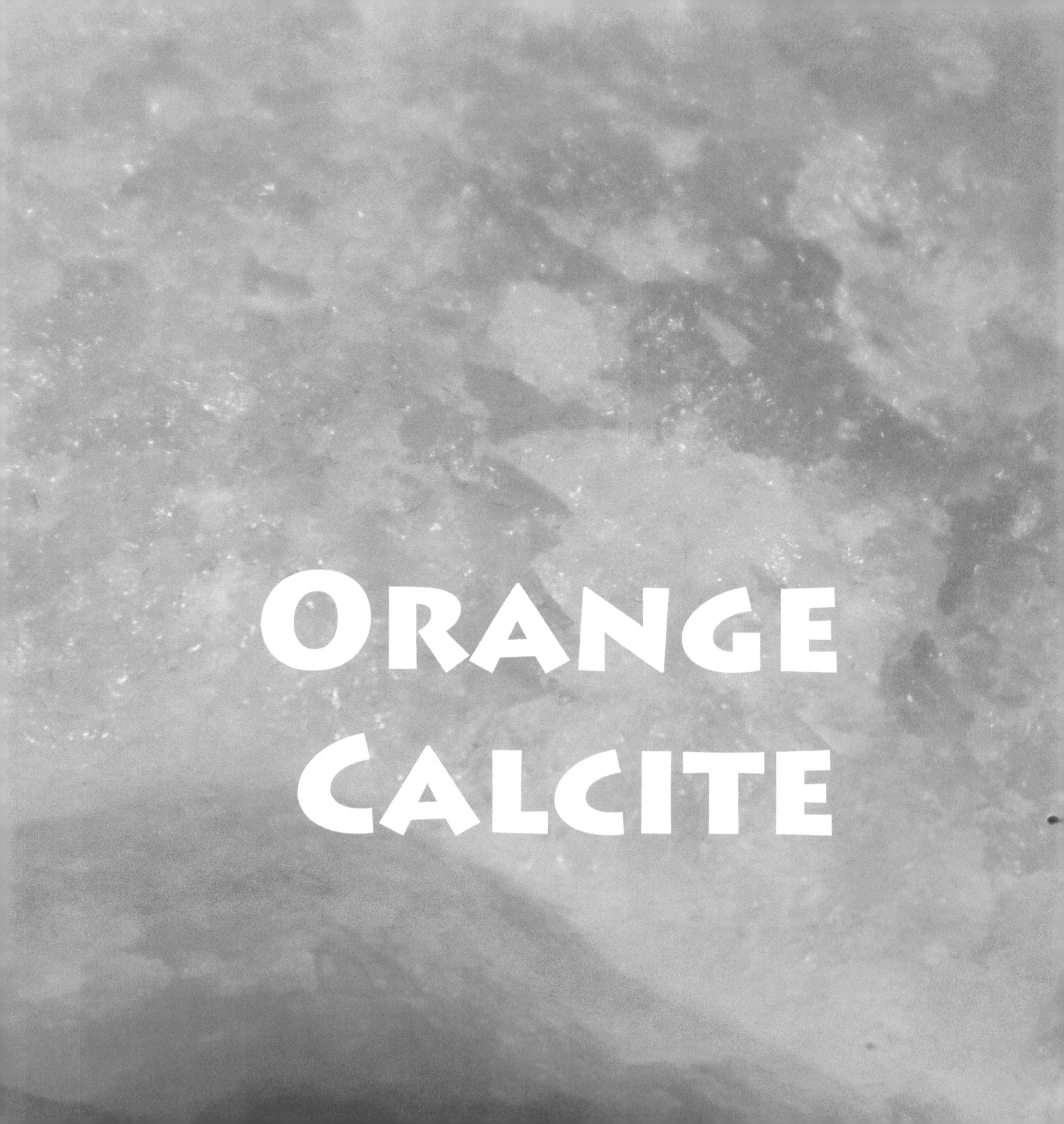
Orange
Calcite

Orange calcite is the color **Orange**.

It can help you to build your confidence.

Is there anything you would like to be more confident in?

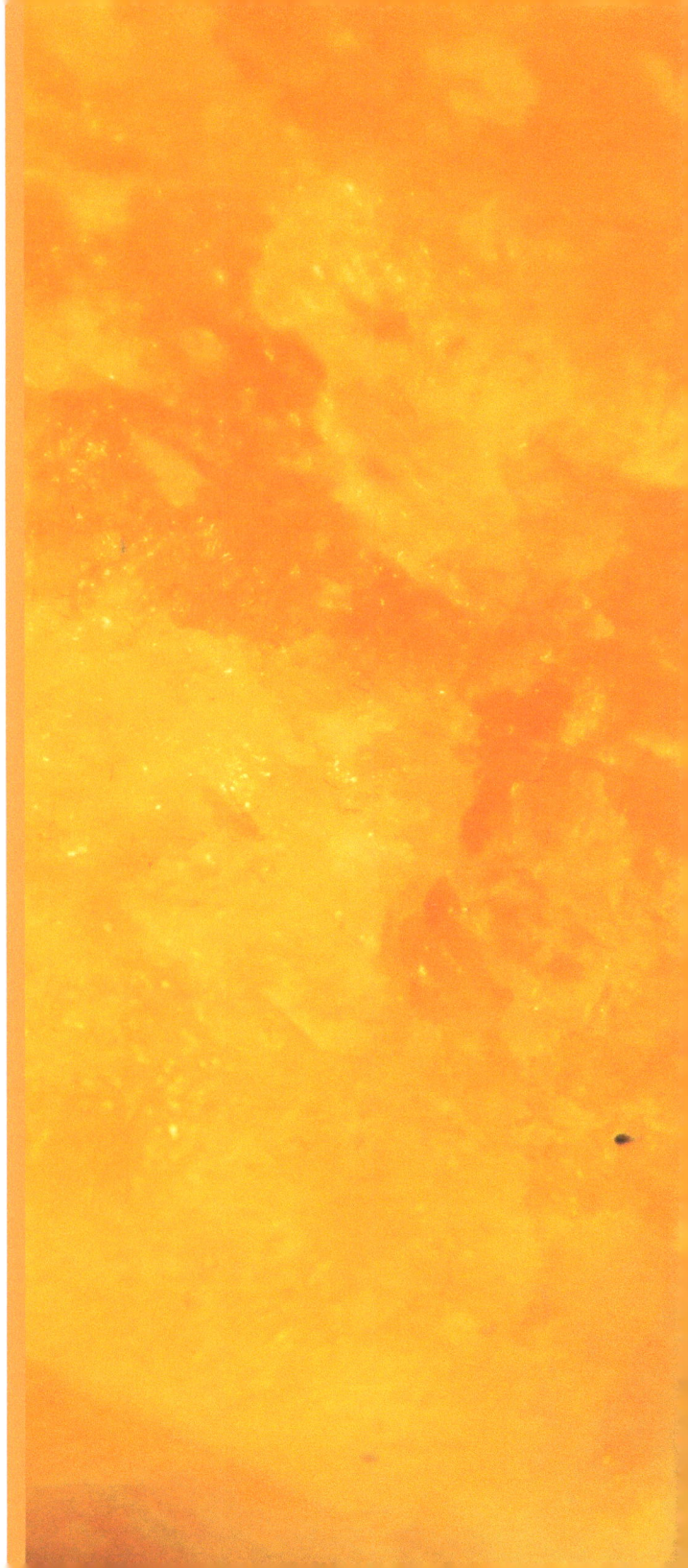

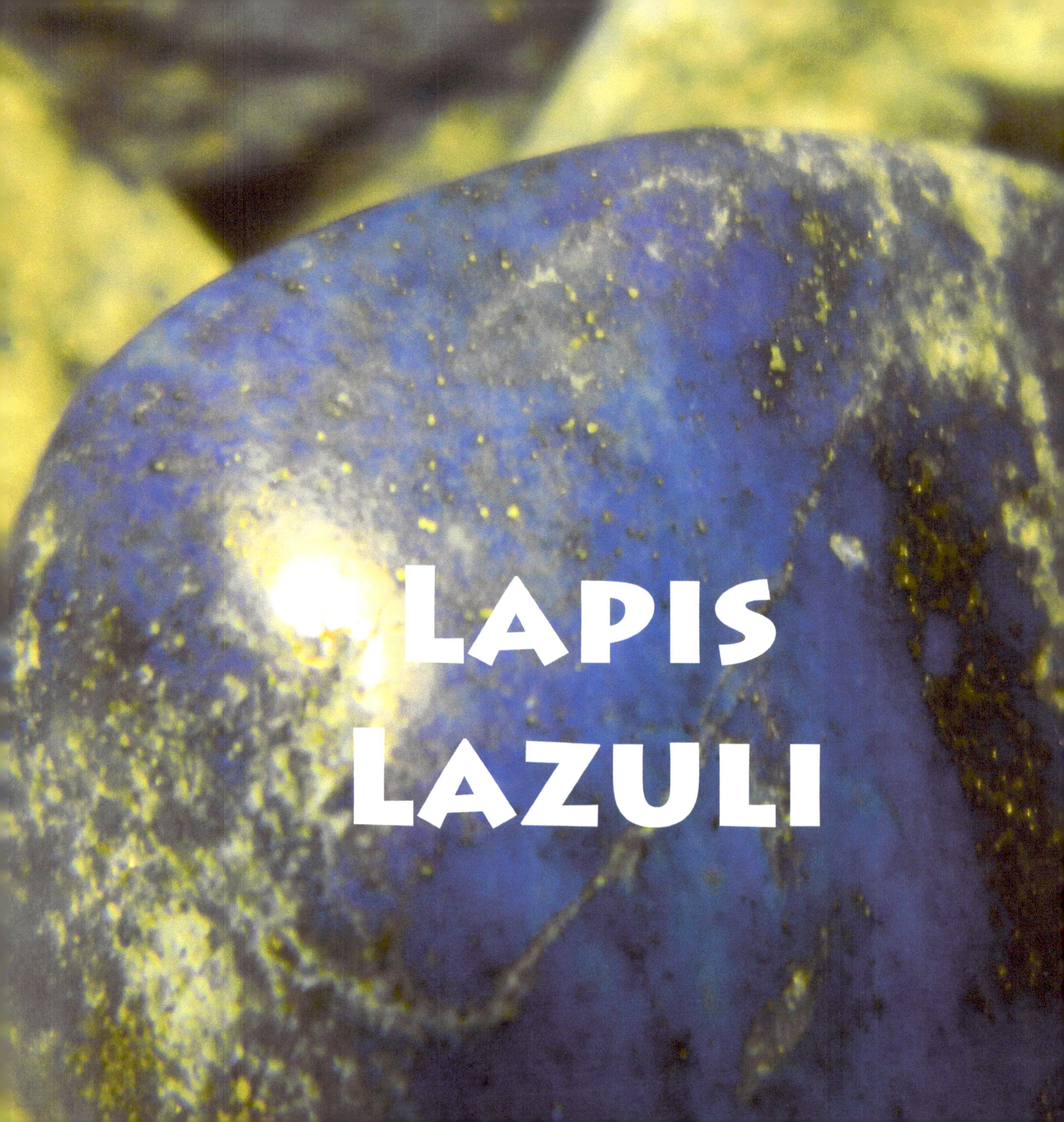
LAPIS
LAZULI

LAPIS LAZULI IS MOSTLY THE COLOR BLUE.

IT HELPS YOU TO BUILD INNER STRENGTH.

WHAT ELSE MAKES YOU FEEL STRONG?

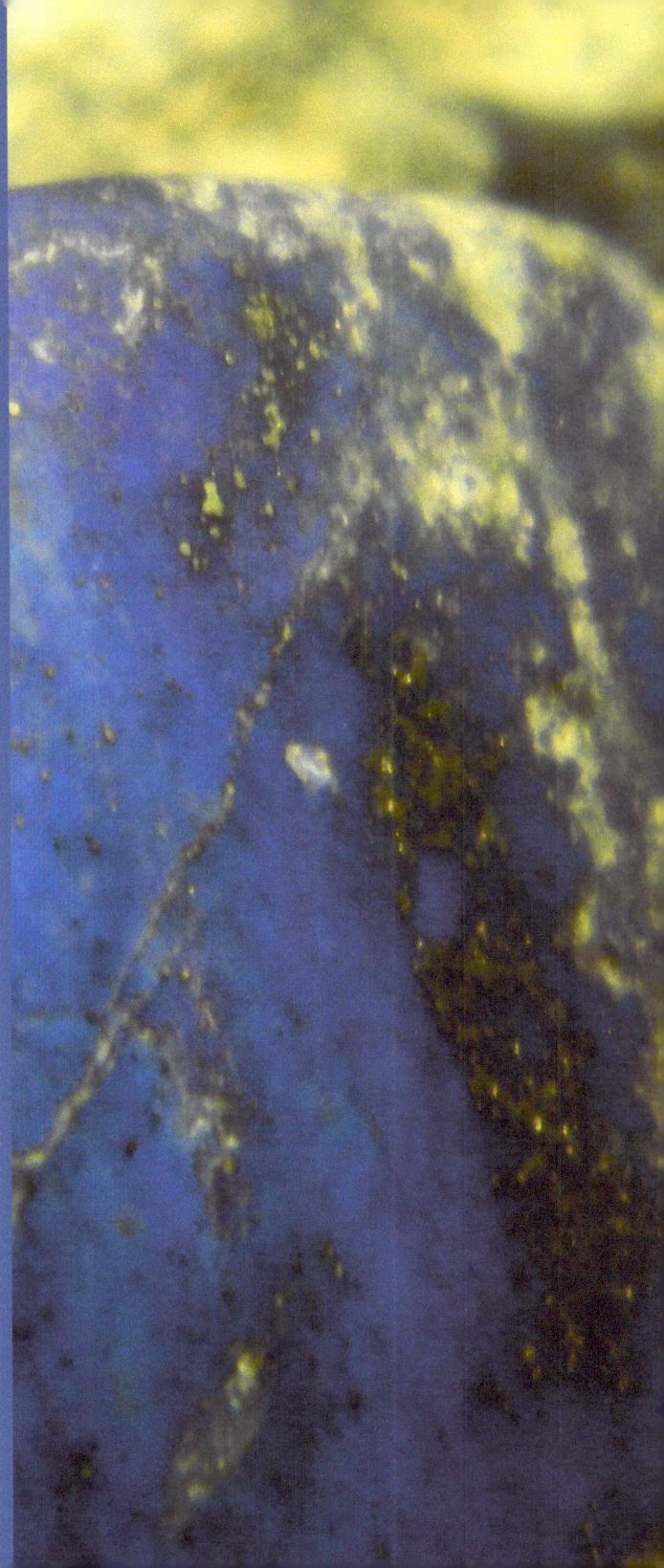

ARAGONITE

ARAGONITE IS THE COLOR BROWN.

IT'S GREAT TO HOLD WHEN EVERYTHING FEELS LIKE THINGS ARE TOO MUCH.

DO YOU EVER FEEL LIKE THINGS ARE TOO MUCH SOMETIMES?

ONYX

BLACK ONYX IS THE
COLOR BLACK.

IT WILL HELP YOU STAY
FOCUSED ON ANY TASK.

DO YOU FORGET WHAT
YOU ARE SUPPOSED TO
DO SOMETIMES?

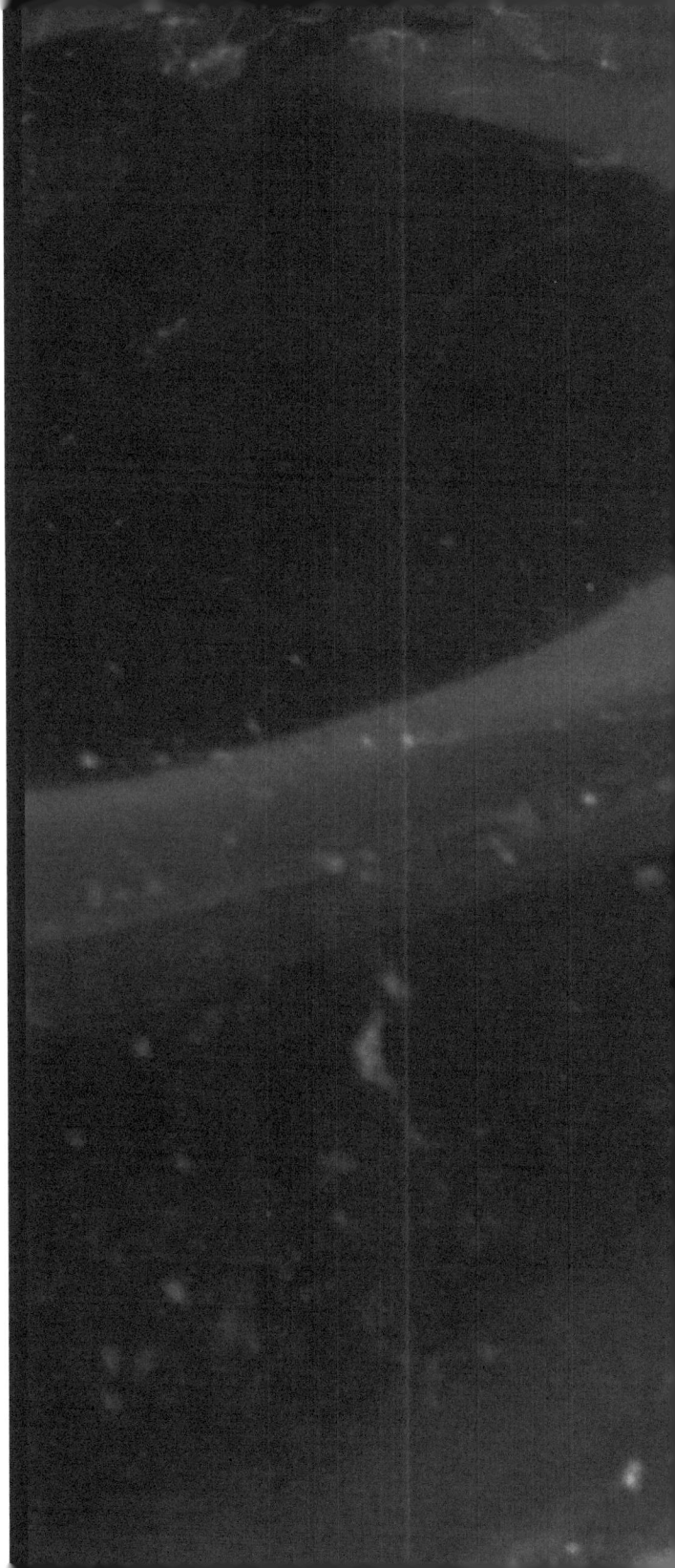

HOWLITE

HOWLITE IS MOSTLY THE the color WHITE .

IT CAN HELP YOU sleep peacefully.

DO YOU HAVE TROUBLE SLEEPING?

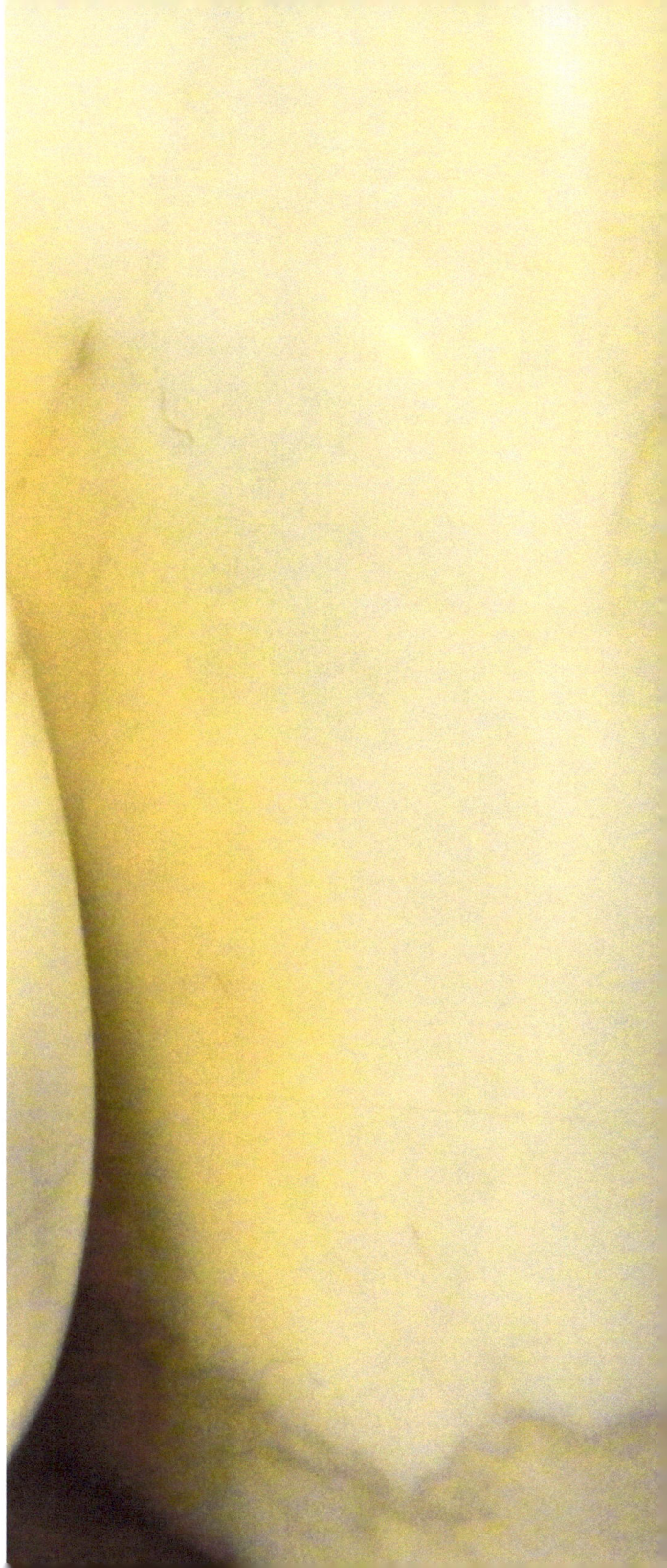

CARBORUNDUM

IS THE COLOR   .

IT CAN HELP WITH PROBLEMS CAUSED BY COMPUTERS.

DO YOU KNOW ANYONE WHO USES COMPUTERS A LOT?

PYRITE

PYRITE IS THE COLOR GOLD.

IT CAN HELP YOU KEEP HEALTHY HABITS.

CAN YOU NAME A HEALTHY HABIT?

ABOUT THE AUTHOR

Nothing is ever happenstance and this life was brought to me
because we asked for each other.

As well as a wife and a mother, I am the owner and creator of
Ori Oasis and OrisOasis.com
For over twelve years, I have done
astrology readings, channeling, oracle readings, as well as
being a mentor to others.

www.ingramcontent.com/pod-product-compliance
Lightning Source LLC
Chambersburg PA
CBHW060853270326
41934CB00002B/124